NATIONAL PARK ADVENTURES...

National Park Adventures...

JOURNEYS THROUGH
OUR NATION'S
GREATEST TREASURES

Julie E. Smith

Julie Etta Smith

"I only went out for a walk, and finally concluded to stay out till sundown, for going out, I found, was really going in."
John Muir

Dedication

This book is dedicated to my wonderful husband Scott whom I share so many of my travel adventures with and also to my three sons: Jeff, Dan and Dave. We have shared many Park adventures together. To all these awesome men in my life I thank you for taking just a "quick" look at all those travel photos through the years. I love you guys. Always.

This book is also dedicated to the memory of my Mom, Evelyn, for her support of my writing. Her encouragement and love inspired me to keep going!

Julie E. Smith

(Cover photo: Cuyahoga Valley National Park, Ohio)

Forward

My interest in the National Parks began to flourish during the Centennial year of the NPS in 2016. In that year, we visited several parks and a westward journey took us to what has become my favorite: Glacier National Park.

Red Bus Tours at Glacier National Park

To get a good overview of Glacier, we started with a bus tour. I sat in the back seat of the classic 1936 *Red Bus* as the driver shifted gears that began grinding in protest as we made our way up the side of the mountain. Even though it was late August, the mountain air was quite cool; I traveled with a woolen blanket across my lap. Gazing out the window, I saw the mountain peaks shooting skyward and many were snow covered. The deep cravasses and valleys among the pine covered mountains held pristine glaciers.

Often our early exposure to park adventures depends upon the parks we live close to. Because I grew up in Iowa, one of my first trips to a national site was Effigy Mounds National Monument. A beautiful park located in northeastern Iowa, it sits atop the high bluffs overlooking the Mississippi River.

My Husband & youngest son hiking the trails at Effigy Mounds, Iowa

This park preserves the ancient ceremonial and sacred sites of Native Americans who built huge mounds in various shapes; mostly animals such as eagles and bears. Over 200 shapes are preserved here and it truly is a sacred space of great beauty. When I first went with my family, as a five year old, I remember walking on the trails and looking out at the Mississippi with my Dad. Decades later, my husband and I stopped there on one of our many trips to Iowa. Our two young sons explored the site: with different eyes, different perspectives.

The NPS Parks and sites have a way of evoking a memory, or creating a story to tell, about one of these diverse and scenic places. Our Parks are the pride of our nation. These Parks have an amazing history with a turbulent past. Seeing the diversity and beauty of what America has to offer makes one want to preserve that feeling.

Everyone experiences the same park or site differently, but gaining perspectives on different parks help you to choose what types of places you would like to visit.

This book is a compilation of the history, geography, stories and helpful hints about enjoying all the National Park Service has to offer. It is not a complete guidebook to each and every park site, but rather, it provides you with an invitation to explore.

I am writing this book to give others an appreciation and an inspiration to seek out many of the beautiful, historical and amazing sights that the National Park Service has out there…just waiting to be discovered. When you see the arrowhead logo, you know you are in for a treat! JES

Contents

1

Chapter 1: History of the NPS

The concept of setting aside land for preservation and recreational use began in this country decades before the National Park Service was established in 1916. The expansion westward and the growth of industry and use of natural resources, with the additional debates of land use, caused much concern over the impact of growth in America. The excitement of new frontiers and endless resources was soon squashed by the reality that both the land and resources on it are not infinite.

Roosevelt & John Muir at Yosemite

Additionally, environmental impacts were not the only item that precluded the establishment of the Park Service. The Civil War had a profound impact on the fabric of how America governs itself. Of course the abolition of slavery was established and equal rights for all people under the law was confirmed (on paper anyway, but it was a start) Yet another concept that came from the Civil War provided for a political change in the country. After the war, the identity of the United States was now more than ever vested at the national level, not the state. State rights were established secondary to federal rights. With this change included the development of several federal institutions, including the establishment of protected parks and protected lands.

On March 1, 1872 Yellowstone National Park in the "territories" of Montana and Wyoming became the first National Park set aside *"as a public park or pleasuring-ground for the benefit and enjoyment of the people."*

Yellowstone not only became Americas first National Park, but the concept of National Parks was lead by Americans and spawned the founding of national parks in other countries around the world. Over 100 countries globally operate national parks. ***But America was the first.***

In the years following Yellowstone, many parks and sites were established and it soon became clear that a system for maintaining and providing for the administration of the parks needed to be created. On August 25, 1916, President Woodrow Wilson signed the act creating the National Park Service to protect the parks and monuments and to ***"conserve the scenery and the natural and historic objects and the wild life therein and to provide for the enjoyment of the same in such a manner and by such means as will leave them unimpaired for the enjoyment of future generations."*** That's quite a tall order and the National Park Service has strived to meet those guidelines.

Many men were instrumental in promoting conservation and the eventual establishment of the National Park Service including (but certainly not limited to) Theodore Roosevelt, John Muir and Stephen Mather.

John Muir has been called the "Father of the National Parks" for his tenacious efforts for conservation and preservation. He was instrumental in formulating many key philosophies regarding land preservation and responsible land use. He developed the model of what a national park should be; and it is still the basic model that is adhered to today by the NPS. He also co-founded the Sierra Club in 1892, the Nation's largest environmental group. He would often journal about his time spent in the wilderness and authored several books. His writings are frequently quoted, yet my favorite is still *The Mountains are calling and I must Go".*

Stephen Mather, an industrialist but staunch conservationist, was named the first director of the National Park Service. During the early years of the NPS, Mather worked tirelessly to help establish the Parks and define them as recreation centers. He also developed the ranger program into a professional curriculum which helped to establish the guidelines for top notch park rangers.

Theodore Roosevelt: The "Conservation
President"

Many men were involved in the movement to protect and establish our public lands, yet Teddy Roosevelt stands out as a key individual in this push of protecting and maintaining these treasured spaces. As the 26th President of the United States, he is often billed as the "Conservation President". His love of the land, and the creatures therein, were evident to those who knew him well, even as a very young man.

His passion for protecting the land followed him into his professional career and his policy making decisions in his Presidency. Roosevelt was instrumental in passing the Antiquities Act , which allowed him to preserve several sites and lands that he deemed worthy of protecting. There was a need to protect several sites that were deemed not suitable for the designation of a national park. During the first three years in utilizing the Antiquities Act, Roosevelt set aside 18 national monuments, five of which ultimately became national parks. Since the fledgling days of the National Park Service, and Roosevelt's push for conservation, the National Parks have weathered many trials and tribulations.

Additions and revisions to those lands that are protected, managed and preserved by the National Park Service are constantly in flux and also how they are managed is often revised.

Brandywine Falls at Cuyahoga Valley National Park, Ohio: one of the newer additions to the National Park Service.

2

Chapter 2: Park or Monument?

<u>Site, Park or Monument?.....Clarification please!</u>

Whenever I visit a place operated by the National Park Service, it never fails....there is confusion among my fellow park goers as to if this is a "Park" or not. A recent visit to the Apostle Islands, a "national lakeshore", prompted me to find out just where the distinctions lie in the park service classifications. It is understandable that there would be some confusion in this arena, because our National Park service manages 419 parks and sites with areas covering over 84 million acres. Within the 419 sites, there are 62 of those that are classified as a **"National Park"**. When people think of the National Park Service, they usually think of just the "biggies": Yellowstone, the Grand Canyon, The Great Smokey Mountains. These are fantastic places to visit, but there is so much more to the NPS than just the 62 parks. Whenever you see the arrowhead logo, you know you are in for a treat. There are just so many things to discover and experience. So for clarification, the National Park Service website (www.nps.gov) has provided a few guidelines to help us understand the classifications:

"--Generally, a **national park** *contains a variety of resources and encompasses large land or water areas to help provide adequate protection of the resources.*

--A **national monument** *is intended to preserve at least one nationally significant resource. It is usually smaller than a national park and lacks its diversity of attractions.*

--In 1974, Big Cypress and Big Thicket were authorized as the first **national preserves***. This category is established primarily for the protection of certain resources. Preserving shoreline areas and offshore islands, the* **national lakeshores** *and* **national seashores** *focus on the preservation of natural values while at the same time providing water-oriented recreation.*

*--***National rivers** *and* **wild and scenic riverways** *preserve freeflowing streams and their immediate environment with at least one outstandingly remarkable natural, cultural, or recreational value.*

*--***National scenic trails** *are generally long distance footpaths winding through areas of natural beauty.* **National historic trails** *recognize original trails or routes of travel of national historical significance.*

Although best known for its great scenic parks, over half the areas of the National Park System preserve places and commemorate persons, events, and activities important in the nation's history.

*--In recent years, **national historic site** has been the title most commonly applied by Congress in authorizing the addition of such areas to the National Park System. A wide variety of titles—**national military park, national battlefield park, national battlefield site,** and **national battlefield**—has been used for areas associated with American military history.*

*--The title **national memorial** is most often used for areas that are primarily commemorative."*

So there you have it…just goes to show you that the NPS is involved in so many ways of preservation, education and recreation for many visitors at a diversity of sites. Another reason the park or monument designations are so important is because policies, funding legislation and land usage can and ARE profoundly affected by the designation.

3

Chapter 3: Trip Planning

Planning a trip to the Parks

There are so many choices and decisions to make when planning a travel adventure to our many beautiful Parks. Yet the decision doesn't need to be overwhelming; different parks provide a variety of adventures…and if you don't like one you can try another. Each Park and site has its own unique characteristics. As you can see from the map below, there is an abundance of places to choose from literally coast to coast.

National Park locations (map from www.mapsofworld.com)

Yet bear in mind this map just designates the major parks, there are several other amazing places to visit with other classifications within the Parks system including protected lakeshores, forests and historical sites. So fear not if there is not Park within a few hours drive of your home, there is bound to be a site with the infamous arrowhead logo somewhere near you.

Once you decide on a destination probably the most important consideration is lodging. The larger and popular parks have many lodging options available; tent camping, RVs and hotels. Since they are popular you would be amazed how quickly they get booked. Depending on the location, you may have to book 6 months to one year in advance. Sounds crazy, right? Yet, if you want the Park experience that you are hoping for, it pays to plan in advance. Our trip to Glacier was in late August and I booked in January. *Score! Got the lodge I wanted.* Some of the Parks have amazing, historic lodges with incredible workmanship. Glacier National Park has three impressive Lodges, each with unique architectural features. The Glacier Park Lodge was built in 1913 by the Great Northern Railroad. It took 75 men a year and a half to construct this amazing building with massive timbers.

Even if you don't stay at one of these impressive lodges, they are definitely worth wandering through the lobby, perhaps having a cup of coffee at a café and perusing the gift shop. The lodges are a bit more expensive than a local hotel, but it's wonderful to at least wander through them and take a look. I actually prefer to instead book a local mid-price range hotel. The trick with that is to find a place just outside the park. If you book inside the Park, it's automatically going to be more expensive. Usually the surrounding towns are able to offer some nice accommodations. Try Google Earth and get a bird's eye view of the surrounding area. It is amazing what you can find with a larger view.

My husband found an awesome ranch and lodge (using Google Earth to search with) right outside Yellowstone that wasn't in any travel brochures. We ended up staying there and YES we went horseback riding. Good thing we went with a trail guide...we are pretty much city slickers! Although one of my sons really took to riding and he looked the part with an awesome hat he bought in Jackson. That was a great trip. It was wonderful being in a forested area, yet only 3 miles from the entrance gate to Yellowstone.

So when planning your trip, take into considerations what activities you would like to pursue. To really get a feel for what each Park has available, a really good start is taking a look at the National Park Service site. They have an abundance of travel tips, maps, historical information and who to contact if you need more information. It's fun just to browse the site to see all that the NPS has to offer. You can find it at: www.nps.gov

Another great source for adventures in the National Parks is this very book you are now reading….good and wise choice. Enjoy your trip to whichever Park you choose, I guarantee it will be memorable.

4

Chapter 4: National Parks Passport

Don't forget your passport!

Seek out and obtain your Passport. Your Passport to the National Parks, that is. It has some of the same concepts as a traditional Passport, you get it stamped at your various destinations, but it is a *whole* lot easier to obtain and contains more information for you than just where you have been. I have visited many National Parks, but just recently obtained my passport at America's *largest* National Park: Wrangell St. Elias in Alaska. Now I just have to "catch up" with all the Park's I visited in the past and fill in the dates. It is fun to cruise through the Passport, finding the places you have seen and remembering the visit. It is also a great partner for assisting in planning your next trip.

The ***Passport to Your National Parks*** program started in 1986, to help travelers in the U.S. gain a broader understanding and appreciation of the treasures of America's National Parks. It serves as a great souvenir to take with you on every trip to "log in" and have your book stamped with the cancellations of the specific park you visited. More than just a souvenir, it has a terrific overview of all the parks and includes maps, color photos and background information on the Parks. The Passport book is divided into 9 geographic travel regions making travel planning and finding specific parks much easier. You can purchase the Passport at just about every National Park, but if you are itching to get a copy right away, you may find it at www.eParks.com

The very informative Program consists of the Passport book, companion books, stamps and the park cancellations. Cancellations for your book are free of charge and are usually available at a park's Visitor's Center. Some people may have the misconception that the "stamps" are affiliated with the Postal Service, as commemorative stamps. This is not the case, they are more akin to large stickers that highlight various features of each given Park: that fit into the Regional stamp sections of the Passport.

Whether you have visited 1 or striving to visit all 62 National Parks, it is beneficial and enjoyable to learn about and participate in the National Parks Passport Program. In addition to providing information about and the locations of each of the Parks, it is good to know that proceeds from the sale of Passports and stamps are donated to the National Park Service. Enjoy the beauty of our National treasure's and.....have Passport, will travel......

5

Chapter 5: Yellowstone

Established in 1872 as the first national park in America, Yellowstone is the Grand Daddy of our national parks. It is interesting to note that not only is it the first in America, it is the first National Park in the world. It is good to be known as a trendsetter for something like this....setting aside land for conservation, recreation and preservation for future generations.

One of the most photographed views at Yellowstone: The Lower Falls

It is an amazing place to visit not only for the historical significance, but the diversity in the features of the park. Yellowstone is quite a popular destination: it hosted 4.12 million visitors in 2018. That sounds like quite a few...but it is a huge park, plus it is not all summertime attendance. Some folks visit for winter adventures, but the most popular times are July and August. A visit to Yellowstone provides a variety of experiences to make it well worth the trip. Included in that list of things to see at the park are: erupting geysers, bubbling hot springs, prismatic reflecting pools, waterfalls and an abundance of readily visible wildlife. All these amazing features are found within this large park of 3,472 square miles. For some perspective, that's more than three times the size of Rhode Island.

Probably one of the most fondly known features of the part is Old Faithful geyser. Like clockwork, it erupts about every 90 minutes. Old Faithful and the many geysers and hot springs serve as a reminder of the unstable nature and changing geology of our planet: especially near Yellowstone.

Also near Old Faithful is a terrific Visitor Information center with all kinds of nifty information about the geyser basin region. Also, if you just missed an eruption, they can advise you when the next one should take place.

Old Faithful Geyser

Just north of Old Faithful are the beautiful prismatic springs and waterfalls. A boardwalk stroll through the various springs gives you a nice view and it's beneficial to try several different viewpoints. One of the most amazing and colorful is the Grand Prismatic Spring. It is the largest in the Park: at 370 feet wide, and stunning to view. If you own a drone for aerial views....this would be an awesome place to try that out!

Grand Prismatic Spring

The wildlife are so accustomed to park visitors; frequently they wander close enough so you can get some awesome photos. Of course that has been known to cause problems, if you don't respect their space and use common sense. They are wild animals after all. When we were near one of the visitor's centers, there was a very large herd of elk that decided to hang out and take an afternoon siesta under the shade of a spreading oak. They are beautiful graceful creatures and several were mothers with young ones to protect. Photos could easily be taken from a safe distance.

Several rangers had carefully arranged some barricades by the sidewalk directly across from the Elk….to keep both the tourists and the elks safe. As you can image, "there's one in every crowd" : some idiot walked over the barricade with camera in hand trying to get much closer for a "great shot." Luckily, he did not get very far before the ranger called out to him. Apparently, he felt he was exempt from following the guidelines put in place by the Park…he just ignored the ranger and kept walking closer. He waved off the ranger who then, justifiably so, got angry. Nevertheless, the ranger's professionalism and manner in handling this incident was incredible. He "hit" him (the inconsiderate tourist) where it hurts: his wallet. The ranger firmly said that if he did not step away he would fine the man $500 for not adhering to Park regulations and disobeying the instructions of a Park Ranger. The elk photographer did back down and I am sure the ranger was relieved that no further action was necessary.

The rangers are there just to protect the beauty and sanctity of the Park, the Park wildlife and to assist visitors in the Park to have a wonderful Park experience. I give all those rangers so much credit; they do incredible work. I have never met a ranger I didn't like: they are all so incredibly helpful and they have a wealth of information about the Parks they serve. Never be afraid to ask questions, they are happy to help!

"Bison Jam" at Yellowstone

On a lighter note about wildlife viewing is a critter you are almost destined to see: the Bison. Yellowstone is famous for its roaming herds of bison. Like many visitors to Yellowstone we were wondering: "What's the difference between a buffalo and a bison?" We wanted to make sure we used the right verbiage for these amazing, massive creatures that you see frequently all around the Park.

Actually, *bison* are the creatures found roaming the American west, not buffalo. Varieties of buffalo are found in South Asia and Africa. A major difference is the presence of a hump. Bison have one at the shoulders while buffalo don't. Buffalo's horns tend to be quite long, bison's horn are shorter. Even with all these differences, it's easy to get mixed up and call them buffalo. Common usage I guess from all those old cowboy Western movies.

In Yellowstone, a frequent occurrence on the roadways is the Bison Jam. Bison, of course, have the right of way and when they want to cross the road, you better let them….at their own pace. We had the excitement of seeing this first hand and you can get some great photos…safe photos…if you use caution and obviously stay in your vehicle.

Heading out west? Be sure to stop at the Grand Daddy of them all: Yellowstone National Park.

By the Yellowstone River in Yellowstone
National Park

6

Chapter 6: Acadia

Cadillac Mountain--Acadia National Park

On the eastern most point of the Maine coastline, atop **Cadillac Mountain,** is one of the places where dawn first touches the continental United States. The 1,530 foot mountain is found within **Acadia National Park,** established in 1919 as the first National Park east of the Mississippi. (Yellowstone N.P. holds the title of the first Park in the U.S.-1872) Acadia is truly a gem on the east coast, a showcase on the Atlantic seashore that Maine residents feel such pride in sharing with visitors to this mountainous part of the state. The park is composed of most of Mount Desert Island and tracts of land on the Schoodic Peninsula and Isle au Haut.

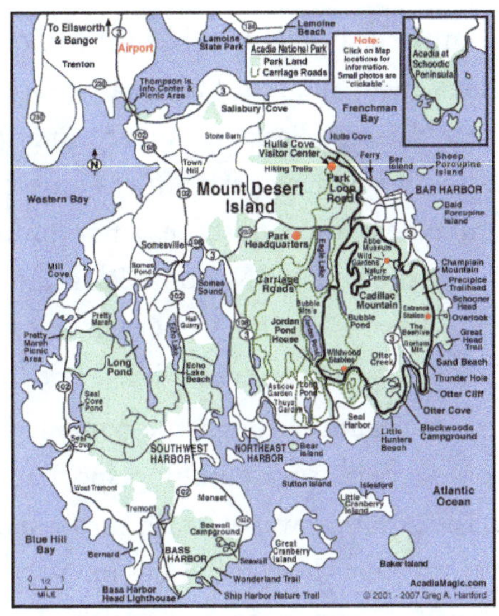

When my family and I visited there, that Maine hospitality and pride of their state is very apparent. My husband's uncle has lived in Maine all his life. He was so delighted to show us around Arcadia and the nearby tourist town of **Bar Harbor.** Being from the Midwest, I pronounced it with the "Rs". A true Maine local would say "Bah Habaw". I probably don't have a correct phonetic pronunciation, but you get the idea...they drop their Rs. On that trip it was a never-ending source of amusement: our Uncle and cousins laughed at the weird sound of our "Chicaawgo" accent and we laughed about Bah Habaw. Bar Harbor is Maine's best-known tourist town, with most of Mount Desert Island's motels, restaurants and shops located there. As you can see on this map, Bar Harbor is right on the coast with a stunning view of the Atlantic, but is just outside the perimeter of the Park. In addition to tourism, Maine is known for being the leader in the Lobster industry. Looking out at the water I remember seeing all the little white dots on the water and then realized that they were buoys designating where the lobster traps were set. A lobster feast in Maine is a must-do while traveling there. The map also identifies many of the incredible features of Arcadia including the carriage roads.

Acadia is a stunning example of a beautiful plot of forested land where the mountains meet the sea. Last year, more than 3.5 million people visited Acadia National Park. Yet don't think for a moment that it feels crowded...the 49,600 acre park affords amble opportunities to stretch your legs and take in the landscapes surrounding you. Although it is considered one of the smaller National Parks, it ranks among one of the most visited. Taking in the scenery is easy by either car or traversing the 125 miles of hiking trails. The ***Park Loop Road*** provides a wonderful sightseeing jaunt through the park. It takes you to Sand Beach, Otter cliffs (a favorite rock climbing spot) and Thunder Hole. At Thunder Hole, the Atlantic waves crash into a narrow chasm with such force that they create a thundering boom. When we went there, my sons were captivated, and impressed by the power of the ocean waves. Depending on the surf, and time of day, the waves rushing in can sometimes create a huge thunder effect and spray water 30 feet into the air.

One of the major attractions of Acadia is ***Cadillac Mountain.*** It is the highest peak in the eastern United States. Reaching the peak by car, is easy from a 3 1/2 mile spur off the Park Loop Road. There are also several hiking trails that end up on the mountain. The view from the top is a fantastic one including the ocean and surrounding islands. Any time of day is beautiful, but a few brave souls take the opportunity to see the first rays of sunlight as it hits the continental shore.

One of the unique features of the Park is the carriage roads. From 1915 to 1940 John D. Rockefeller financed, designed and directed the construction of the carriage roads. The roads provided access to the park by horse-drawn carriages and were banned for usage by automobiles. The carriage roads still prohibit automobiles and are treasured by hikers, bikers and horseback riders. The roads include 17 hand-built granite bridges, each a beautiful addition to your travel throughout the park. The preservation of the carriage roads is also a unique tribute to John D. Rockefeller, as he was the one that donated land to the National Park Service to provide for establishment of the Park.

Being the lighthouse lover that I am, I would be remiss if I did not mention one of the most photographed lighthouses that happens to be in the Park at the southernmost tip of Mount Desert Island: ***Bass Harbor Light***. It sits atop a perilous looking cliff and the tower height itself is 32 feet; relatively short for lighthouse standards but its light extends far out into the Atlantic. The lighthouse was built in 1858, and became fully automated in 1974. Probably one of the most photographed because of its location on a majestic pine-covered cliff overlooking fantastic sunsets on the Atlantic. Definitely photo worthy.

Bass Harbor Lighthouse

Acadia National Park is New England's only National Park and a beautiful Park preserving the forested lands and the rugged cliffs of the Atlantic seaboard. For more information you can contact: http://acadiamagic.com or the National Park Service site information at: www.nps.gov/acad/index.htm

7

Chapter 7: Glacier

Stunning view of mountains & Goose Island at St. Mary's Lake

During the centennial year for the National Park Service, 2016, a campaign called *"Find Your Park"* was run to encourage visitation to the many choices available in our national park system. I feel it is hard to narrow your choice to ***just one*** favorite park, but nevertheless I have *"Found my Park"*: Glacier National Park in Montana. The only thing I can see wrong with the park is for me it has become an obsession...I can hardly wait to return. It was originally on my "Bucket List", and I am so very happy I was able to visit the Park, but I really hope to return again someday. I left the park with a desire to return because it is so vast and with an abundance of adventures, that you really can't experience Glacier all in one trip.

Glacier National Park is located in the northwestern corner of Montana, bordering Canada. The Park was originally established in 1910 and encompasses over 1,500 square miles. The range of topography in the park, including mountains, crystal clear lakes, glacial feed streams and forested valleys, provides not only a photographer's dream but also numerous other recreational pursuits. The park is home to 762 lakes and several waterfalls-both big and small. In addition to kayaking, canoeing and fishing, there are 151 maintained trails in Glacier for many different hiking experiences. The Park also supports a large population of both plant and animal life. Bears, both black bears and Grizzly, are among the mammals found here. An abundance of Big horn sheep and mountain goats are also found grazing on the highest peaks.

Another unique feature of Glacier National Park is that it has been declared the world's first International Peace Park. At the northern boundary of Glacier, the border into Canada connects with Waterton Lakes Park. The two parks together share over 1,800 square miles of breathtaking summits, glacial terrain and shimmering waterfalls. I had hoped to see Waterton as well on my trip. My husband and I both took our passports (yes, required) however we ran out of time. Perhaps on my next trip. Also, the area is home to many Native American tribes and the Blackfeet Indian Reservation is on the east side of the Park.

A very good place to start at Glacier, to get an overview of the entire park, is the iconic **"Going to the Sun Road".** The road bisects the park, traverses up and over mountains and crosses the Continental Divide. It was a monumental task to complete and took 10 years build; the road opened in 1933. Personal vehicles are allowed on the road, but I recommend leaving the driving to the experts: the drivers that are familiar with all the *sharp* turns and heart stopping drop offs. If I had to drive it myself I would have been "white-knuckling" it the entire way and would have not been able to enjoy the views. If you are a seasoned mountain driver, go for it...I'm from the Midwest: a true flat-lander when it comes to driving. So my husband and I decided to take a **"Red Bus Tour"** and it was incredibly well worth it.

The Red Buses themselves are a staple in the Park and have a rich history. Since 1914 the Red Bus Tours have been operating in Glacier and providing for visitors *"unparalleled experiences touring through one of the most spectacular*

Red Bus Tours: Classic tours at Glacier

parks anywhere, and they have done it with the elegance and grace that has become synonymous with these unique vehicles."

I thought it was a nice touch that all the drivers wore a dress shirt, tie and a "motoring cap". The buses themselves were made by the White Motor Company around 1936 and then refurbished by Ford Motor company. Logos for both companies are on each vehicle. Several different tours are available: some 3 to 4 hrs, others all day (8 hrs). If you are visiting Glacier I would highly recommend a Red Bus Tour and I stress the importance of a reservation. It is a pretty popular activity in the Park and they get booked. For more information, their website is: *http://www.glaciernationalparklodges.com/red-bus-tours*

Glacier Park
Lodge-built 1913

Another historic and stunning feature of Glacier are the historic lodges of the Park. When planning a stay near Glacier, there are an abundance of lodging opportunities available from bed & breakfasts, camp grounds and several hotel chains. Even if you choose to stay somewhere other than the classic Lodges you've **just got to go see** these beautiful iconic lodges.

Go have a cup of coffee or lunch or just peruse the little gift shops. There are four beautiful historic Lodges at the Park: Glacier Park Lodge (built 1913), Many Glacier Hotel (1914), Lake McDonald Lodge (1913) and St. Mary Lodge and Resort (built early 1930's) All of the Lodges were built in the grand, old style of a mountain resort with huge pillars, taxidermy mounts and several windows to take in the views of beautiful mountains and pristine lakes.

Originally named Glacier National Park, back in 1910 there were about 100 glaciers, sadly that number has diminished to 37. It is a changing world we live in and Yes you can blame mankind, in part anyway, on climate change. However, in the bigger picture the climatic changes we experience are also evolutionary changes on our fragile planet. Whatever the case may be, I highly recommend going to Glacier National Park and soaking up all the beauty you can experience there...get there before they all melt. It may be sooner than we realize.

8

Chapter 8: Boston

Boston is a city that stands as a shining example of the blending of old and new elements. Boston is steeped with history showcasing the birth of our nation and the events of the American Revolution. Yet, in the same token it is a modern bustling city with glimmering skyscrapers next to the shores of the Atlantic. There is so much to take in when visiting this east coast city and there is something to appeal to every taste: history, architecture, diverse cuisine, beautiful parks and of course the famous *Freedom Trail.*

Even if you have never been to Boston, the **Freedom Trail** is the most talked about and highlighted feature of the city. The red brick pathways throughout the city streets lead you to 16 of some of the most significant events in the history of the United States. And yes, they happened in Boston. Boston is frequently referred to as "The Cradle of Liberty". The trail was originally conceived in 1951; the trail was completed and by 1953 40,000 people were walking the trail annually.

The trail is easy to follow by the narrow red bricks marking the way. The entire trail is only 2 1/2 miles long, but to take it all in perhaps its easier to walk part of the trail and "trolley" part of it. There are two trolley companies within the city that provide "hop on, hop off" service. I would highly recommend this, it's an easy way to get around and see the sights you want to without becoming completed exhausted. They both have web sites and information on their tours: **Old Town Trolley Tours** and **City View Trolley Tours.**

Red brick pathways marking the
Freedom Trail

One of the best places to start learning about all the ins and outs of the Freedom Trail is with the **National Park Service.** The **NPS** provides an abundance of information detailed the significant events of the birth of our nation. The **National Park Service** has two Visitor's Centers in Boston: one in Faneuil Hall in the heart of government center area and the other by the harbor and the USS Constitution. We went to both Centers and both facilities offer an abundance of information to gain a better understanding of the historical significance of all the sites along the Freedom Trail. For those of you who are NPS passport holders, like myself, I am thrilled to report there are 16 different stamps you can collect from all the historic sites. I didn't get all of them, but added quite a few to expand my Passport collection.

Quincy Market-built 1826

In the heart of the city is a vibrant market place housed in both *Faneil Hall* and *Quincy Market.* Faneil Hall was built in 1742 to serve as a central market but town meetings were also held here from 1764 to 1774. Samuel Adams led meetings here with protests against the taxation of the colonies, when some of the first stirrings of a revolution began. Today Faneuil Hall contains shops and restaurants on the first floor, the NPS Visitor's Centers on the second floor and a museum on the third floor. The museum contains a collection about the Ancient and Honorable Artillery Company of Massachusetts. The Company was founded in 1638 for defense of the colony. The display has occupied space in Faneuil Hall since 1746.

In the same courtyard as Faneil Hall stands the stately building with Greek columns: *Quincy Market.* It was named after the mayor of that time period (1823) who pushed to have the marketplace built to accommodate the needs of the growing city and the overcrowding at Faneuil Hall. Quincy Market was completed in 1826. It is a fascinating place to visit with all the sights and sounds of a thriving marketplace. Fish, meat, cheeses and an abundance of produce are seen up and down each aisle displayed by a diversity of vendors. Not only is this harbor town known for their wonderful seafood, but Bostonians have a unique accent and are not shy about it.

Just take a look at this sign at a seafood vendor I saw at Quincy Market, it really gave me

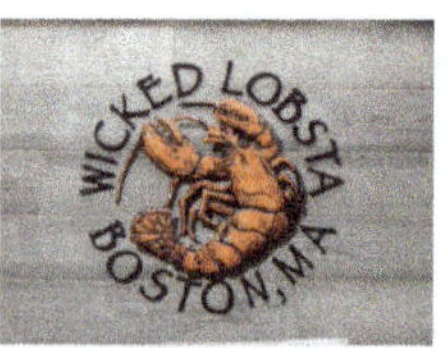

In Boston, we love
Lobsta

a chuckle. The way to pronounce Lobster is to drop the R....Lob-sta...that's the Boston way. I love it.

We enjoyed talking with the locals and their accent was very evident with the trolley drivers. Perhaps they ham it up a bit for the tourists. I know that our Mid-western accents sound quite odd to them. That is always a fun part of traveling about the country. It's English, but there are just so many different ways to speak it. Additionally, in this same marketplace, there are two additional buildings: **South Market** and **North Market.** Wow....So much shopping, So little time.

One of the highlights on the Freedom Trail takes you to the Charlestown Navy Yard; where the Charles River meets Boston Harbor. Here sitting in the harbor, is the oldest commissioned U.S. Naval ship: the **USS Constitution**. She really is quite a sight to behold, and looking at all the rigging on her sails, it's hard to imagine all the sailors operating them without tripping over each other. It would definitely have to be an orchestrated effort.

USS Constitution

The ship was built by Bostonians and launched in 1797. She sailed in 40 battles and never lost one. She was nicknamed "Old Ironsides" because of the way cannonballs would bounce off her tough oak planking. When visiting this sight, you are allowed to walk on the ship and explore it. However, security is tight because part of the facility is a working Navy base, it's not all for tourism. The museum on the premises is also very interesting, it's hard to take in all the information at one time, perhaps warrants multiple trips.

The oldest public park in America, the Boston Common, is in the heart of the city and provides lush green spaces, manicured walkways trimmed with flowers, a small "frog pond" and a larger lake. It was originally established by the Puritans in 1634. Within the park is a beautiful pond with the infamous Swan Boats floating gracefully across the pond.

The boats are as quiet and gently moving as a real swan, because there are no motors; powered only by peddling of the swan boat "captain". Even when filled with people, the whole park is serene and a lovely place to relax on a blanket on the grass.

Swan Boat in
Boston Common

Another charming aspect of the park is the adorable ***"Make Way for Ducklings"*** statue that pays homage to the classic children's story by Robert McCloskey. The tale of the wayward ducklings was inspired by the busy streets of Boston and a Mama Mallard trying to protect her brood. It was originally published in 1941, but its continued popularity has held the test of time as a classic children's story.

"Make Way for Ducklings!"

Crossing the bridge on the Charles River, from Boston to Cambridge, takes you to two of the most prestigious institutions of higher learning in America: Harvard University and MIT. Harvard holds the title of the oldest college in America, it was founded in 1636. Today Harvard also is known as a leading research facility. The Massachusetts Institute of Technology (MIT) was founded in 1861 and has become one of the world's leading technical institutions.

Boston is indeed a city of many *"firsts"* in our county. The first printing press was in Boston in 1638. The first subway was in Boston, 1898. The first World Series was held in Boston, 1903. The last "first" I will mention is near and dear to my heart: The Boston Light was the country's first lighthouse in 1716. How could I have missed that when I was there....sounds like I need to head back to Boston for a personal photo of that iconic lighthouse.

The Boston Light- America's first:1716

9

Chapter 9-Olympic

Olympic National Park, located on the western edge of Washington state, showcases three distinct ecosystems: a rainforest, a wild flower meadow and a rugged Pacific shoreline. The exotic terrain and beauty of these systems are all showcased in the 1,441 square miles of this park located on the Olympic Peninsula. When visiting there, it's a bit perplexing to understand the "boundaries" of the park because the terrain is so varied and part of the park follows the coastline of the Pacific ocean with a seemingly endless horizon.

The trees in this park are wondrous and their sheer size takes your breath away. Walking among these trees gives a mere human a sense of the grandeur of all creation and at the same time the fragility of our beautiful planet. Some of the tress are hundreds of years old and can reach a height of 250 feet, with some having a circumference of 30 to 60 feet. Going on a walk in these woods helps to give perspective on the connectivity of life, all life. John Muir, the naturalist who was one of the men instrumental in helping to create the National Park Ser-

Huge pines in the Hoh Rain Forest

vice said simply: ***"The clearest way into the Universe is through a forest wilderness."*** (John Muir, 1938) It's amazing that this is one of the few rain forests in the lower 48 states. A key feature that allows this rain forest to thrive is the abundant rain. Precipitation in the Olympic's rain forest ranges from 140 to 167 inches per year. Luckily, we happen to time our trip there on a sunny, warm day.

The park that is next to the Pacific boasts two beautiful beaches that stretch along the Olympic Coast National Marine Sanctuary: Rialto Beach and Ruby Beach. Rialto Beach is further north and Ruby beach is south near the Hoh Indian Reservation. These are not the kind of beaches you park yourself on a beach blanket with a margarita in hand; they are very rocky, rugged with a ferocious surf. Nevertheless they are wonderfully scenic and you can spend hours beachcombing to see amazing shells, driftwood and view the iconic "sea stacks" by the shore.

Sea Stacks at Ruby Beach

Sea stacks are steep columns of rocks formed by wave erosion. Along this particular beach, the sea stacks create quite an interesting and diverse view along the shoreline.

With the strength of the pounding surf, the driftwood that decorates the beach more closely resembles art sculptures in a variety of shapes. Art inherent in nature. Some photographs depicting close up views of the huge logs show the detail and the resulting effects of wind and water. Everywhere you look, from every angel...there's something new to discover, and to photograph!

Entering the park is probably easiest from Hwy 101 by Port Angeles. The main Visitors Center is located at this entrance and the untamed beaches on the Pacific side may also be accessed from Hwy 101. Also by 101, situated at the northernmost area of the Park, is the amazing Lake Crescent. The glacial formed lake waters reflect a beautiful azure color, have very limited algae growth and are crystal clear. Some days you can see 60 feet down into the lake that has been measured in places at 624 feet deep. The lake is the perfect environment to support several different types of trout. When we visited the lake, we didn't have the opportunity to go fishing, however we were able to have a peaceful picnic lakeside. Also on the lake is the historic lodge: Lake Crescent Lodge. It was built in 1915 and each of the rooms has a view of the lake. This is one of three historic Lodges found in the Park.

The beauty of Lake Crescent: Glacially
formed and up to 624 ft. deep!

Olympic National Park is a gem in the Pacific northwest that definitely warrants a visit when in the area. I have only been once, but would love to visit again someday.

10

Chapter 10: The Badlands

Visiting the beautiful Black Hills and the Badlands of South Dakota, travelers often wonder why it is called The Badlands. Badlands National Park in southwestern South Dakota is only one area that holds the title of "badlands". It is a geologic term that describes landscapes characterized by soft sedimentary rocks. This type of terrain can be found all over the west in places like Wyoming, Utah, North Dakota, Colorado and Nebraska.

Surveying the rugged terrain at
Badlands National Park

The Lakota people were the first to call this place *"mako sica"* or *"land bad"*. French Canadian fur trappers called it *"les mauvaises terres pour traverser"*, or *"bad lands to travel through."* When one surveys this barren, rocky terrain with limited moisture and vegetation you can see why the title stuck. Nevertheless, the rock formations and colors in the sedimentary rock create a surreal landscape that seems not of this world. The famous architect, Frank Lloyd Wright was impressed with the uniqueness of this land. In 1935 he wrote:

"I've been about the world a lot and pretty much over our own country, but I was totally unprepared for the revelation called the Dakota Bad Lands...What I saw gave me an indescribable sense of mysterious elsewhere-a distant architecture, ethereal...an endless supernatural world more spiritual than earth but created out of it."

So I would agree with Mr. Wright: the Badlands create an other world atmosphere...sometimes you feel you are wandering on a different planet. The different textures and the way the sun light and clouds plays across the horizon make the rock structures seem to go on indefinitely. When I was there with my family, I remember one of my sons commenting that it felt as if we were "walking on Mars".

Yet even with this desolate terrain, there are a variety of creatures and plant life that are abundant here and call this territory home. The prairie and rocky terrain amazingly are able to support 60 different species of grasses.

Watch your step on the trail!

This in turn provides a food source for several animals including bison, prairie dogs, coyotes, snakes, vultures and bluebirds. When we were there, we did not see much wildlife...or snakes thank goodness...but this is the first sign we saw on the trail. Good to know!

In addition to the living creatures, this region is rich with fossilized remains of a variety of creatures. In this desolate place, it's intriguing to think that many of the fossils are of aquatic dinosaurs. When the formation of the Badlands began, over 75 million years ago, there was a shallow sea spanning from the Gulf of Mexico to Canada encompassing the Great Plains area. The creatures sank to the bottom of the sedimentary layer and became fossilized. All the different layers of rock also provide a geologist's dream and include: sandstone, silt, mudstone, limestone, volcanic ash and shale. These layers create a multi-dimensional and colorful landscape.

Many travelers heading to South Dakota and points west catch sight of the popular destinations of Mount Rushmore, Devil's Tower's and many more in that neck of the woods. Yet, the eerie and majestic beauty of the Badlands is worth adding to your trip agenda. For more information check out the National Park Service link to The Badlands: https://www.nps.gov/badl/index.htm

11

Chapter 11: Grand Teton

"In and around the lake, Mountains come out of the sky and they stand there" --Roundabout by YES

The Teton Range: Grand Teton National Park, Wyoming

Looking at the majesty of the Tetons, I was reminded of those lyrics by the band YES from so many years ago. I have always liked that those words seem to bring the mountains to life. A life of their own and as they stand there, if they were so inclined they could get up and walk away to another place.

The Teton range has been "standing there" for millions of years, but was established as Grand Teton National Park in 1929. About 13 million years ago, two blocks of the earth's crust shifted on a fault line, tilted one up and the other down forming the range we view today. The highest peak: "Grand" reaches to a height of 13,770 feet.   The area surrounding the range includes a lush valley with crystal shining lakes, groves of aspen trees and alpine meadows. The park is 484 square miles and includes the range and most of the nearby area of Jackson Hole. Not to be confused with specifically the town of *Jackson, Wyoming.* This flat valley surrounded by the towering mountains was visited by many trappers in the 1800's. The area was named "Jackson's Hole" after Davey Jackson: a trapper from that time. In time, the apostrophe was dropped and it just became Jackson Hole. Both the town of Jackson and the geographic namesake of the area are linked historically and are "next door neighbors" sharing the same inspiring landscape.

Many visitors to the Park also spend time touring the town of Jackson and many hotels, restaurants and shops are found closely to the Park. Jackson is also the home to three popular ski resorts, so it is even busier during the winter months. We were there in summer and there were some visitors from the Park, but their peak season is ski season. When we went to the Grand Tetons, we stayed in Jackson and had the opportunity to explore both.

One of the most unique features of Jackson was the Town Square: decorated with cowboy statues and arches made from antlers. On first view, it seems a little morbid...but come to find out the elk shed their antlers every year. Most of the antlers used in the construction of the archways were collected from the area in the woods. Otherwise, that would have been quite a few elk to shoot! Here's a photo of one of the arches. They do have quite an impact: it gives the town square a real rustic, western feel.

Antler Archways, Jackson

There are three entrances to the Park, the southern entrance is only 4 miles north of Jackson. If traveling from the north, via Yellowstone National Park, the two parks are only 31 miles apart. Nevertheless, the Tetons are frequently overlooked by the notoriety of Yellowstone. Both parks have their own unique features, but personally I liked Grand Teton better. The majestic beauty of the mountains and the quiet solitude of the shimmering lakes gives one a wonderful sense of calm...good Zen. Yellowstone provides a great showcase of unique geographic features: erupting geysers, bubbling mud pots and breathtaking waterfalls. I don't deny these are all part of an awesome park adventure, but the majesty and serene landscapes of the Tetons should not be missed.

Jenny Lake-Grand Teton National Park

With the varied terrain there are also different hikes suited to different skill levels. Yet, the easy to moderate level hikes provide a great day hike through sparkling streams, alpine meadows and loads of photo opportunities. We took a relatively short hike and ended up at Jenny Lake. Since it was an easy hike, we were not alone on the trail, but not crowded by any means. I am always amazed by delightful conversations with fellow park goers. We had asked two women if they could take our family photo and they were happy to oblige (most folks usually are...) Come to find out they were also from a Chicago suburb; very close to where we lived. Small world.

Some of the most iconic photographs of Grand Teton National Park include the antique barn on Mormon Row Historic District: the Moulton Barn. The barn stands as a picturesque back drop to grazing bison and antelope. It

Moulton Barn on Mormon Row -Grand Teton National Park (photo by PhotoJeepers)

also reminds the viewer of the challenging life of farming that took place on these rugged lands. The area was settled by Mormons in the late 1890s. The community was established and 27 homesteads were built to form a close knit community. Most of the farmers grew hay and oats and had limited livestock. In the mid-1900s, Mormon Row was acquired to expand Grand Teton National Park and in 1997 the district was added to the National Register of Historic Places. Several iconic barns still stand today and are widely recognized in photographs with the Teton range as the backdrop.

Grand Teton National Park: a magnificent, must see park for travelers in the western U.S.

12

Chapter 12: Theodore Roosevelt (North Dakota)

Theodore Roosevelt National Park-south entrance near Medora, N.D.

As one drives through the rugged terrain of Theodore Roosevelt National Park, you appreciate the beauty of the rugged cliffs and eerie colors formed by the diversity of minerals found in this land. Land that has remained untouched by plows or backhoes for centuries, only modified by the wind, the sun and torrential rains. Included within the park are a diversity of landscapes and geological formations, such as the Petrified Forest and Painted Canyon. The park consists of three separate units: the South unit (right off I-94), the North Unit and Elkhorn Ranch Unit. Each portion of the park offers an abundance of things to explore and opportunities for viewing wildlife. Since the South unit is easily accessible (Exit #24 and #27 from I-94) near Medora, ND and also has two Visitor's Center to help plan your adventure within the Park, it has a tendency to be the more frequently visited area of the Park. The Visitor's Center also has a really interesting museum about the man, the legends and some of the "naked truths" about this fascinating man who became our 26th President. I was saddened to learn that Roosevelt lost both his mother and his wife on the same day: Valentine's Day, 1884. I can't imagine the overwhelming grief. He did seek solace in the lands that he so loved in the hills of North Dakota. These hills in this area are classified as "Badlands" and the simple beauty here can be found as sedimentary rocks carved out by glacial rivers rise among the prairie flowers. An occasional tree spots the landscape, but the grasses and flowers are abundant.

The "Badlands of the North"

Theodore Roosevelt National Park, located on the western side of North Dakota, is a more low-key National Park and does not boast huge mountains or erupting geysers, but nevertheless it is an amazing landscape that has been called *The Badlands of the North*".

Not only does it help to protect this unique area of land, it also pays homage to a man who played a huge role in the development of the National Park Service that we know today.

It is fitting that North Dakota was chosen as the site for Theodore Roosevelt National Park. This land truly inspired him and helped him grow and toughen his resolve, both physically and mentally. He first came to North Dakota in 1883 to "bag a buffalo" and later become involved in ranching. Through a series of both bad luck and severe weather killing the majority of his livestock, he gave up the ranching life. However, the lessons he learned in the wilderness and with cattle ranching helped to strengthen his resolve and also helped to solidify his conservation ethic. He was quoted as saying: *I have always said I would not have been President had it not been for my experience in North Dakota.*

Roosevelt and John Muir at Yosemite

Theodore Roosevelt was sometimes referred to as the "conservation President". He was responsible for establishing five National Parks and also created a system for the President to preserve lands and monuments by the creation of The ***Antiquities Act*** of 1906. Roosevelt signed the act into law, which gives the President of the United States the authority to, by presidential proclamation, to create national monuments, protect public lands and to protect significant natural, cultural, or scientific features. Roosevelt's first use of the Antiquities Act was to declare the unique feature of Devil's Tower in Wyoming a National Monument. The Act has been used over a hundred times since its passage. Its use occasionally creates significant controversy, usually instigated by differences of opinion between Congress and the President.

So here's to those that help to preserve the beauty of our America. Hopefully, Roosevelt's passion for the parks and conservation can inspire us all to enjoy what the parks have to offer. Additionally, he was a great example of being a champion for preservation and advocacy of some of our Nation's impressive resources. Thanks, TR...hopefully we can carry the torch.

13

Chapter 13: Cuyahoga Valley

**Boardwalk path to Brandywine Falls,
Cuyahoga Valley National Park**

Many people don't realize it, but there is a beautiful "gem" of a National Park in the heart of the Midwest, just south of Cleveland Ohio: ***Cuyahoga Valley National Park.*** From the Native Americans word for "crooked river", it is pronounced "Ka-uh-ogh-ha". It is a beautiful park with waterfalls, cliffs and valleys, and a rich history about life in the mid-western states. When people think of National Parks, they frequently think of the "classics": Yellowstone, Acadia, the Grand Canyon. Yet this park in Ohio is a beautiful representation of our National Parks system: preservation of natural beauty and also a link to the past.

Looking at timelines, Cuyahoga Valley National Park is very young as a member of the National Park service. It was established as a National Recreation Area in 1974, then became a National Park in 2000. The fact that it is a relatively young National Park is very evident as one drives through the park and sees many residential areas throughout the park that were "grandfathered" in and allowed to remain within the park boundaries. These private residences do not distract from the beauty of the park, however sometimes seem odd from what people consider a "National Park" should be like. There are so many roads that go in and out of the park, and of course the residents that live there have easy access in and out. It sometimes blurs the definition of the park boundaries.

The park itself preserves 33,000 acres along the Cuyahoga river valley between Cleveland and Akron, Ohio. The natural beauty of the park includes deep gorges, waterfalls, cliffs and century old majestic trees that rise high in the

Bridal Veil Falls

skyline. Most of the trees are typical of the Midwest and the deciduous seem to outnumber the pines. With the abundance of Maples, I would imagine this would be a wonderful place to visit in the Fall to see all the changing colors. A diversity of beautiful wildflowers can be found throughout the park and more than 100 bird species nest in the valley. The many trails within the park are perfect for both hiking and biking. Many cyclists make use of the fantastic "towpath trails" that follow the canal paths throughout the park. Some of the canals have all but disappeared except for a low trench, but others still have water in them and still seem "usable". The towpaths where the mules were used to tow boats along the canal, have all been resurfaced and make fantastic bike paths.

Canal boats pulled by mules

In additional to the natural features, the park has a fascinating history about the use of the canals. The "canal era" from roughly 1825 to 1913, was a period of time that Americans relied heavily on the use of the canal system for economical transportation of both products and passengers. The Ohio-Erie Canal was built in 1825 and served to connect Lake Erie all the way south to the Ohio River. It helped to provide transportation and increase commerce from 1827 to 1913. In 1913, a devastating flood occurred that did extensive damage to the canals. At this time the railroads were also expanding into a major form of transportation and beginning to replace the widespread use of canals. The railroads soon became the primary source of transportation and life on the canal boats became a distant memory. When visiting Cuyahoga Valley National Park, be sure to visit the **Canal Visitor Center**, in the northern part of the park with some fascinating displays and some really interesting historical information about river commerce and lifestyles of the hardworking people who depended on the canals.

Another aspect of the park that is rich in history, and also provides an adventurous way to get back and forth throughout the park is the **Cuyahoga Valley Scenic Railroad.** The train ticket gives you an all day pass and you can get off at any stop and get back on to explore several areas within the park. The train also offers meals onboard and "tastings" of beer or wine. With your tasting, you receive a CVSR commemorative tasting glass! Cyclists can also board the train, with their bikes. They have the option to bike the towpath trail one direction then take the train the other. Considering how many lengthy trails there are in the park, this is a terrific option for cyclists if you just run out of steam. Bear in mind that the train does not run 7 days a week. Unfortunately when I was there it was not running. Generally they run Wednesday through Sunday, but be sure to check their web-site for more detailed information and ticket prices: http://www.cvsr.com

Like many National Parks, the park rangers are so interesting to talk with and have a wealth of information about the attributes of their park and also the area of the country they live in. At CVNP, it is no different: the rangers are happy to provide a wealth of information about the natural and man-made history of the park. Since this is a relatively young park, perhaps they are even more excited to share with you how this park came to be. Cuyahoga Valley National Park truly is an interesting gem of a Park to visit in the Midwest.

Chapter 14: The Mighty 5: Utah's National Parks

The "Mighty 5" in Utah are National Parks that provide such grandeur, stunning landscapes and outdoor adventures that they surely are befitting of the description: Mighty. Starting from the southwest corner of the state and moving eastward they are : Zion, Bryce Canyon, Capitol Reef, Canyonlands and Arches.

Zion National Park (photo: Dept. of Interior)

It was in just this particular order that we traveled, starting our journey with Zion National Park and making our way eastward. It is amazing that when you view all the parks on a map clustered together in the same general vicinity it would seem easy to visit them all within a short time…not so. Utah is a relatively large state and the vastness of it is complicated by the fact that there are fewer roads to take you from point A to point B. I'm not complaining; it's wonderful to have the spanning horizons unscathed by roadways. It just takes longer to visit if you want to do justice to all 5 Parks.

Out of the Utah National Parks, Zion is the most visited National Park; in 2019 the Park received 4.5 million visitors. Canyonlands, however is by far the largest Utah park with 337,598 acres. All five Parks have their own distinct geographic features and breathtaking views, but the mountains of Zion and majesty of their height really diminishes the height of a small human being as one stands in awe. Especially for a Mid-westerner like myself, who is not accustomed to being around mountains like this. A couple of times I found myself gazing upward with my mouth agape: "Oh…Wow!"

Although Zion National Park was established in 1919, it has only been in recent years that the popularity of the park has soared. The Parks further north of Zion (the favorites of Yellowstone and Yosemite for example), had become traveler's favorites. Yet, all the amazing pathways to be explored at Zion have brought many travelers through the gates. There are of course, pros and cons to this expanding appreciation of the Park. It is nice to have people love and appreciate the Park, but sometimes managing crowd control and assuring the preservation of the Park can be a challenge.

When we were there, our country was in the midst of a pandemic. In October of 2020, after months of quarantine, everyone was wanting to get outside and many of the National Park Service sites saw a surge in attendance. Several things were not "normal" and I do give the Parks administra-

Waiting for the Zion shuttle; with masks and social distancing

tion credit for doing their best to assure a safe and healthy environment. One example, was limiting the shuttle buses to 50% capacity so as to improve social distancing. This was a great idea...but did create long lines to get on a shuttle and limited how much you would have time to see in the park.

Getting tickets for the shuttle in advance is a whole other story...yikes! They are only $1.00, but you have to have one to get to certain areas of the Park. I know they had to institute a ticketing procedure for "crowd control"...but it was very frustrating. My advice for trips to a popular National Park such as Zion is plan MONTHS ahead of time. I booked our hotels in January for an October trip. Shuttle tickets, campgrounds and other reservations can be found on http://recreation.gov .

Zion National Park is situated on part of the Colorado Plateau and the sandstone cliffs, towering mountains and river valleys provide a stunning remnant of how this part of the continent was formed roughly 250 million years ago. Looking at the vastness of the terrain, it is hard to imagine that this land was once submerged in a shallow sea and this area was considered part of the super-continent of Pangaea. As a hiker kicking up dust and stones along the path, it is compelling to think how this terrain has evolved through both erosion and tectonic shifts. The canyons and sandstone cliffs provide unique and colorful views. Zion National Park helps to preserve the most sacred and impressive canyon country and wilderness ecosystem on our planet.

One sight, and hike, that I did not attempt while at Zion is the infamous Angels Landing which rises 1,500 feet above a sheer wall face above the Virgin River. There are chains bolted into the rock face in part of the walkway to provide "security" on your walk. Just looking at the photos of a chained walkway on the side of a mountain scared me to death. Well, guess what...when we got there the Angels Landing trail was closed because of the pandemic. (whew...wipe brow with relief), Now I don't have to come up an excuse not to go. Apparently, it was too hard to assure "social distancing".

Trails by the Virgin River

However, my son and his friends went on another challenging hike that Zion is famous for: The Narrows. It is what the name dictates; where the canyon Narrows and is carved out by the Virgin River. The trail is mostly wading through the cold water anywhere from ankle to waist deep. The entire trail is 16 miles long. Many hikers just go part of the way and turn around; it is a very arduous hike and very tough in water with the uneven terrain of the river rocks. Our group all made it back in one piece.

Before you enter the Narrows is a beautiful, easy hike: Riverside Walk that follows the Virgin River. Part of the walk is paved and the rest is a groomed path that is easy to navigate. My husband and I enjoyed our time on that path while waiting for the guys that had ventured into The Narrows.

After departing Zion, and with a sad goodbye to our son and his friends, we started heading east while they headed west back to San Diego.

Our next stop was Bryce Canyon National Park. It is the smallest of the Mighty 5 parks, but has a huge impact visually. Technically it is not a canyon, but rather a series of amphitheaters cutting into the pink/red rocks with spires rising up skyward. The rock spires, called hoodoos, are an intriguing example of how erosion and freeze/thaw cycles have molded the rocks.

Another story about the hoodoos is told by the Paiute people in the area. They tell of the Legend People who were animal-like people. They behaved badly and treated Coyote so badly, that he turned them into rock formations. The creatures huddled together and still stand as when they were first turned to stone. The impressive and ever-changing hoodoos and other rock formations seem to be the highlight of the park, but the dense forests and sporadic meadows provide a serene setting.

Since the park's elevation ranges from 6,000 to 9,000 feet, its usually much cooler here than at the other Utah parks. When we were there, the heavily forested sections in the park made me feel, briefly anyway, I was back in the great north woods of Wisconsin. The terrain of course is very different than the Midwest, each region having their own distinct characteristics and shining attributes.

Hoodoos at Bryce Canyon

After leaving Bryce, our next stop was to Torrey, Utah. We stayed at Cowboy Homestead Cabins: cozy, very nice and situated close to the entrance of Capitol Reef National Park. The Park's namesake comes from the presence of several white rock domes that resemble the U.S. Capitol. Also a huge geologic feature in the park is water trapped in the pockets of rock creating a "Waterpocket Fold" and hence the creation of a "reef". Early explorers, in the 1870s, found it difficult to navigate and started referring to this unique geologic feature as a "reef". The Waterpocket Fold extends 100 miles from Thousand Lake Mountain to the north all the way south to Lake Powell.

Prior to the arrival of the Mormon settlers, the Native American Fremont people lived in this area. Several examples of their rock art have been preserved on petroglyphs. The art is an amazing depiction of the hunting and gathering lifestyles of the Fremonts. Capitol Reef was one of the last places in the West to be explored by immigrant settlers.

Mormon style farm settlement-Capitol Reef National Park

It was not until the late 1870's when the Mormons began settling into the region. The town of Fruita was established and many of the orchards that were planted and irrigated still exist today. The National Park Service still maintains the orchards and visitors to the park can enjoy many "pick your own " crops of cherries, peaches, pears and apples. Unfortunately we had just missed the apple picking season when we were there. Yet, in Fruita we made a stop at the little country store (very quaintly fashioned after a 1900 farmhouse) and had hot coffee with one of the biggest and best cinnamon rolls I have ever tasted! The turn of the century barn, blacksmith shop and split rail fencing all around the area, gives one a real feel for life as a southern Utah settler in the early 1900's.

After Capitol Reef, our journey took us to Moab, Utah. Very interesting place that I found out is a real mecca for dirt bikes, mountain bikes and ATVs. I can't blame them…all those awesome trails with jumps, racing curves and are naturally groomed by nature. I did not pick Moab because of this however…the town of Moab is centrally located to both Arches National Park and Canyonlands National Park. Great location and the town itself has several great restaurants and overnight lodging.

Our journey to Arches was short lived. We made it to the entrance and got the traditional "sign picture", then I saw several vehicles driving toward the gate, then turning around. Then I saw it: a light-up sign with the message: "Park Full"—"Turn around Ahead". Needless to say I was disappointed, but not too terribly surprised since we were visiting in the age of a pandemic and were experiencing firsthand the limiting of park visitors. I am sure Arches is a popular park, and they have to assure that it won't be too crowded…but still, I was very sad at the time. Arches is known for a stunning collection of over 2,000 sandstone arches. Additionally, the landscape includes an amazing array of balanced rocks, pinnacles and spires. Most of the formations are red sandstone. You can image my disappointment when we did not make it past the front gate. Maybe next trip.....

Well, even though we didn't make it to all of the Mighty 5, three out of 5 ain't bad and it gives me motivation for a return trip. There are many sights to take in while visiting Utah.

"Delicate Arch" at Arches National Park...probably one of the most photographed images in southern Utah. (photo from findmymojyo.com blog)

15

Chapter 15: The Alaska Parks

Alaska beckons. The mountains are calling. The pines whisper and the frozen tundra holds curiosities beneath. The unique lands showcased in the parks there demonstrate its reputation as The Last Frontier. Alaska is a youthful state, gaining statehood in 1959, but the marvels of this land are timeless. There are 8 National Parks and 16 National wildlife refuges in the state of Alaska making it the leading state in the volume of protected lands.

Horseshoe Lake at Denali National Park

Like much of the state, Alaska's parks and lands live up to their reputation as being the "Last Frontier". The breathtaking beauty of the forested lands, the snowcapped peaks and the diversity of wildlife is showcased in the parks. Yet, because of the ruggedness of the land, some of the places are very hard to get to and are not frequently visited. That could be good or bad depending on your perspective. Out of the eight National Parks in Alaska, I have visited three of them; as it turns out the three that are the most accessible.

Probably the easiest to access and one of Alaska's most popular attractions is **Denali National Park.**

Denali is Alaska's most well-known national park and is actually more readily accessible than some of the other remote parks. Denali averages over 400,000 visitors annually. The flag ship feature of the park is the 20,320 feet high mountain peak known for thousands of years by the Athabascans as Denali, or "The High One".

Denali in the Fall--NPS photo by Tim Rains

So What's in a Name? The park we know today as Denali National Park was founded in 1917 by Woodrow Wilson as Mount Mc-Kinley National Park. The name of the Park has been a controversy since its inception. There are certain ironies that one can't help but ponder on. First, the name Mc-Kinley was taken from our 25th President William McKinley. McKinley himself had never traveled to Alaska. Perhaps he would have gone to see the majestic mountain and park, but sadly he was assassinated in September of 1901. Charles Sheldon, a naturalist and conservationist, advocated from the start the name of Denali for both the park and the mountain. The locals called it Denali, and the debate continued for decades. Finally in 1980, many continued to favor the name Denali after the Alaska National Interest Lands Conservation Act changed the park's name to Denali National Park and Preserve. But the official name of the mountain remained Mount McKinley. Then just prior to the National Park Service centennial year in 2016, the mountain was reverted to the name *Denali.* While visiting Alaska in September of 2015, President Barack Obama announced the official name change of the mountain.

Keeping the "wild" in Alaskan wilderness. The vastness and diverse ecosystems of the park are beautifully preserved and presented to visitors by virtue of how the park is operated and maintained. Unlike other National Parks, access into the park is restricted and controlled by only one road, 90 miles long into the park. Personal vehicles are not allowed beyond the 15 mile mark on the park road; only the shuttle buses taking visitors back and forth from several destinations. This may seem odd at first, but when you take a bus trip into the park it helps you to understand how this system helps to minimize car travel and reduce the carbon footprint on this wilderness. Riders are free to get on and off the bus as they please. Another distinct advantage is that you are much more likely to view an abundance of wildlife. The animals have become accustomed to the big tan buses along the road and are more likely to view them as just a part of the landscape. When we went, we observed, from the safety of the bus, a mama Grizzly helping her two cubs to hunt a ground squirrel. That was an experience I will never forget.

In addition to the park road, the trails allow foot traffic within the park for both the casual hiker and the seasoned veteran. Some of the more seasoned hikers are encouraged to "make their own trail", but for the casual hikers there are several trails starting closer to the Visitors Center. An easy hike, 1.5 miles, to the beautiful plateau above *Horseshoe Lake* provides ample opportunities for stunning photographs.

Wildlife thrives in the vastness of the park and the *"Big Five"* have been designated as: grizzly bears, wolves, moose, caribou and Dall sheep. It may be a personal goal to view all five, but don't be too disappointed if you don't view them all. You can always pick up a coffee mug or t-shirt with all of them on it; sounds a bit touristy but a great way to remember your visit.

Photo from: thebudgetsavvytravelers.com

My family and I saw a grizzly and her cubs from quite a distance and also a mother moose and her cubs, but sometimes it's very cool to also capture them on a souvenir. Not quite the same as seeing them in real life, but it's so neat to bring back the memories of your trip and be able to say you've been to Denali. Wolves and grizzlies are not as easily seen, but the abundance of Moose in the park makes it almost a sure bet you will see them at some point. Depending on the year, the moose population within the park fluctuates of course, but the National Park Service estimates about 1,800 Moose at Denali. That's alot of Moose! Just FYI, the plural of Moose is Moose...good to know.

Visiting with one of the sled dogs of Denali

"Mush, Doggies! Mush!" You can't get up close and personal with a grizzly, but at Denali you can get close and cuddly with the sled dogs. In the winter months, the best way to get around from here to there within the park is still by sled dog team. One of the *must see* attractions at Denali is the sled dog demos and a visit to the kennels. Even if you are visiting in the summer, they have to keep the dog's training going year round, so they add small wheels to the sleds to

run them on all terrains. During the summer tourist season, they have 3 daily dog sled demonstrations. The Park Service runs several shuttles to the kennels. When I was there I was amazed to find out the importance of the use of dog sleds within the park and also within the state of Alaska. The most famous, well -known sled dog race, the Iditarod, has a colorful and intriguing history. Portions of the Iditarod trail were used as early as the 1880's, However the most famous event in the history of Alaskan mushing is the 1925 serum run to Nome; also known as the *"Great Race of Mercy."* A large diphtheria epidemic threatened Nome. The only way to get the antitoxin to Nome was by sled dog, due to unusable planes and ships in the worst of winter. So on January 27, the port at Seward had received the serum where it was passed to the first of twenty mushers and more than 100 dogs who relayed the package 674 miles from Nenana to Nome. The dogs ran in relays, with no dog running over 100 miles. Wow, I hear that story and am amazed of the courage and tenacity of those mushers and their dogs. No wonder it has become an inspiring tale; both for those that participate in the Iditarod and those that watch on the sidelines. All an amazing part of the Alaska experience.

Another very accessible Alaska park , via Seward, is **Kenai Fjords National Park** . It covers about 950 square miles and showcases some of the iconic features of Alaska including glaciers, marine life and coastal scenery.

A large majority of the Park is either in the waterways or frozen icefields, so one of the best ways to get an overview of the park is via a tour boat from Seward into Resurrection Bay and parts of the Gulf of Alaska. There are several tours available from the starting point

Kenai Fjords National Park--Photo from Major Marine Tours, Seward

of Seward for both wildlife viewing and fishing excursions. We went

on an afternoon cruise with Major Marine Tours. Getting out on the water gives you a great overview of one of the crowning features of the Park: the Harding Icefield. It is 70 miles long and 30 miles wide and creates all the glaciers in Kenai Fjords National Park. It is incredible to see-and hear- the glaciers "calve" icebergs into the bay by releasing massive chunks of ice into the water.

Puffin--(photo by Major Marine Tours)

Additionally, on the boat tour, we were able to see numerous examples of Alaska marine life. We saw Stellar Sea Lions, Bald Eagles and an abundance of Puffins and Kittiwakes. Puffins were always my favorite. They look so cute and pudgy and seemingly awkward, but they are fast flyers and divers with excellent fishing skills.

Another aspect of our tour at Kenaj Fjords was my first introduction to the concept of the "Land of the Midnight Sun". Since we were there in August, the long days and short, short nights were very evident. At the end of the tour we came back to the harbor, pulling up to the dock and the sun was still high on the horizon. It felt like about 6 or 7 pm, but it was 10 pm. So odd. Now I know why residents of Alaska purchase "black out" curtains to get a good night sleep. Yet, as a tourist it's great because you can fill so many things in one day and you don't run out of daylight.

The only road in the Park, ends at the Exit Glacier parking lot. From there you can take an easy hike to view the glacier face. It is one of the most accessible glaciers in Alaska and terrific to view, but sadly is also a very visible indicator of glacial recession due to climate change.

Exit Glacier near Seward. Photo taken in 2017; shows how far the glacier has receded past the 2005 marker (photo: Dan Smith)

Another impressive Park that holds such beauty, but is somewhat more challenging to journey to is ***Wrangell- St. Elias National Park and Preserve.*** It is on the eastern side of the state about 250 miles from Anchorage.

Wrangell- St. Elias is a vast national park that holds the title of the largest of our national parks at 13.2 million acres. To provide some perspective, the park is the same size as Yellowstone National Park, Yosemite National Park, and Switzerland combined! The combined mountain ranges in the park: Wrangell and St. Elias contain 9 of the 16 highest mountain peaks in the U.S.

The Largest National Park:
Wrangell-St. Elias

Also within the Park reside the remnants of the historic Kennecott Mine and a very interesting visitor's center explaining what life was like in the glory days of copper mining. It's a fascinating place to visit because it is a demonstration of the tenacity and ingenuity of the human spirit. When traveling the McCarthy Road to get to the mine, you feel as if you are already on an adventure, and you sometimes have to reach into your own resolve when seeking this destination.

The McCarthy Road is 60 miles long and is a long gravel road. Here is a photo showing where the nice smooth pavement ends and the gravel road & imposing cliffs begin. It is intimidating when all the travel literature warns NOT to take rental cars on this road and other warnings for the faint of heart.

Adventures awaits:
The McCarthy Road

It was a rough ride with several portions of the road demonstrating the "wash-board" effect, a series of tight ridges. I give my sister-in-law, Christy, so much credit: she drove both in and out on this challenging stretch of road. We took her mini-van, which worked well and we took it slowly. That is the key to surviving on this road without a flat tire or worse damage to your vehicle. It is only 60 miles, but plan for about 3 hours. It is well worth the trip if you take your time. You can see so much more when you are traveling at 30 mph as opposed to 65.

Be sure to catch all the scenery and wildlife along the way and the views are spectacular. The amazing Kuskalana Bridge, built in 1910, spans 525 feet and sits at a height 238 feet above the river. An incredible building accomplishment and yes we drove across it. Having a little bit of a fear of heights (don't we all to some extent) I had to hold my breath and somehow muster up the courage to take in the view. Be courageous and take in the view, it's worth it.

**Kennecott Copper Mine,
Alaska--operated from 1900-1938**

So travelling along the rustic McCarthy Road, you eventually meet your destination: the McCarthy/Kennecott settlement and the Kennecott Mine. Nestled in the snow capped mountains of the Wrangell-St. Elias range, the Copper Mine was closed in 1938. It stands silent watch above the valley and the steep drop offs that are common to the area.

When visiting the abandoned mine, the sheer majesty of its size gives you a whole new appreciation for the people who lived and worked here. The structure of the main mill has such an ominous presence that even if it is not haunted it still has an alarming presence that truly is awe-inspiring. The building of the mine itself, and the surrounding buildings supporting the workers, initially seemed to be insurmountable tasks. To bring buildings materials in through the rugged mountain passes, the first priority was to build a railroad. In addition to helping construct the new city and mine, the copper ore was transported via railroad south to Cordova. When visiting Kennecott, I walked along the original rails that line up with the chutes, where the rock crusher spit out processed rock and ore that was further refined.

Remnants of the tools that were used in the labor intensive process of mining are found strewn about the area. Here my son Dan surveys the rugged Wrangell Mountains while standing by an ancient rock crusher, circa early 1930's. Also remnants of the life that was left behind after the mine closed are

View of the Wrangell Mountains

still visible and one gets a strange sensation that memories and spirits of the past still are present here. It seems to have had more recent activity in the mine than the footsteps of tourists and it is hard to believe it closed more than 75 years ago. Nevertheless, as one of those tourists, I found it a fascinating historical place to visit and taking in the natural beauty of the park was an inherent bonus.

The National Park Service acquired the mine in 1998 and the lands of the historic mining town of Kennecott. The mine has been designated a National Historic Landmark. On the Wrangell-St. Elias website: www.nps.gov/wrst life working in the mine is described: *"Kennecott was a place of long hours and hard, dangerous work. At the height of operation about six hundred men worked in the mines and mill town. Paying salaries higher than those found in the lower-48, Kennecott was able to attract men willing to live and work in this remote Alaskan mining camp.....Despite the dangers and grueling work, the Kennecott workers mined and concentrated at least $200 million worth of ore."*

The mine successfully ran for over 30 years, but was closed due to declining copper deposits and the high cost of railway maintenance.

It would be quite a challenge to see all eight of Alaska's parks, yet even taking the opportunity to visit a few definitely gives you an appreciation for this most beautiful land. Alaska is full of breathtaking vistas, welcoming people and places that create memorable trips of a lifetime.

16

Chapter 16: Follow the NPS Arrowhead

Every time you enter the entrance gate of a National Park, a historic site or walk in the serene beauty of an area preserved by the National Park Service, you will see this arrowhead sign. The sign tells you, of course, that this is a site operated and maintained by the National Park Service. Yet, it also tells you that you are about to explore something that has been deemed worthy of protection and also so intriguing that it needs to be shared . I have reached the point with so many NPS Parks and site visits, that my enthusiasm for all things NPS related bubbles over when I first see the arrowhead sign…I know I am in for a treat! However, not only a treat, but also surprises at discovering new and different things. The variety of places to visit within the scope of the National Park Service never ceases to amaze me. There is always something new to explore.

There are currently 62 National Parks in the United States, but actually 419 protected *sites* which include such areas as lakeshores, forested areas and significant historical sites. So many times, travelers think they need to visit the "big" Parks to really experience what the National Park Service has to offer. The well known Parks are incredible....no denying that, but it is nice to explore some of the intriguing sites in your own back yard. When I first moved to Wisconsin, I was delighted to find out that a Visitors Center for a NPS protected site was only about 20 miles from my home: the *St. Croix National Scenic Riverway.*

I have been there several times and I always learn something new. A trip to the Visitors Center is a great way to learn how the St. Croix and the Namekagon rivers have had an incredible influence on this area of the upper Midwest. In addition to learning about the fascinating geologic and historical information of the area,

St.Croix River-border between Wisconsin & Minnesota

one can also get information here on hiking, canoeing and fishing these beautiful waters. The rivers have provided commerce, recreation and also abundant resources to support a diversity of wildlife. The rivers of the St.Croix and Namekagon together make up 252 miles of protected waterway in the St. Croix National Scenic Waterway.

The geologic history of the area began millions years ago when the glaciers carved out the river valleys and rugged bluffs overlooking the flowing rivers. The first human inhabitants of the rivers were the Dakota(Sioux) and the Ojibwe (Chippewa) that found this area to have plentiful resources for an abundant life. The next to explore this area were the French and later the English fur trappers.

The logging industry in the area took the St. Croix river valley by storm and the pique of the logging industry was the 1890's. Log jams in the river frequently occurred, not only hindering the progress of lumber to the mills, but also damaging the fragile ecosytems of the rivers. The life of the lumberjacks was challenging on the river, to say the least, and many lost their lives in this profession.

St.Croix River logging: early 1900's (photo: National Park Service)

They built small shanties that floated in the river to help carry supplies and were sometimes used to sleep in as they were "steering" the lumber downstream. The shanty was called a *Wannigan* as shown is this photo. The last major log drive was in 1914. It is interesting that in St. Croix Falls, WI. and Taylors Falls, MN. the lumber industry and the rich heritage of the river is still celebrated today with "Wannigan Days". Now that is neat! I learned that new tidbit of trivia when moving to this area....I bet not that many people know what a Wannigan is, well know you know.

The St.Croix River Visitor Center is easily found at 401 N. Hamilton Street, St. Croix Falls, Wisconsin. It is just off the main road (87), 2 blocks north of the deck of the St. Croix Overlook.

Another example of an NPS site very close to my "own backyard" that I discovered is the Apostle Islands National Lakeshore on Lake Superior. Located near Bayfield, Wisconsin they are a series of 21 islands in Lake Superior that are protected by the National Park Service.

"Sea Stack" in the Apostle Islands

Sea Caves, Lighthouses, Shipwrecks and breathtaking Sunsets.....all these amazing attributes are found among the islands above the northern tip of Wisconsin in the chilly waters of Lake Superior. These unique islands were sculpted out of sandstone and formed towards the end of the glacial period 10,000 years ago. The amazing colored agates and rocks found in the area were deposited as the glaciers melted.

Many stories surround how the Apostle Islands got their names, but the commonly agreed upon one, involves the biblical parallel to the 12 Apostles. Early explorers to the area were missionaries and tended to name new areas based on Biblical names. Counting the islands loosely, many believed that there were only 12, so the name: the Twelve Apostle Islands seemed appropriate. Even though there are 22, the name **Apostle Islands** remained.

It's interesting that there are only four areas protected by the National Park Service as "national lakeshores" and the Apostle Islands is one of them. President Nixon signed the bill establishing the **Apostle Islands National Lakeshore** in 1970. There are 22 islands in the Apostle Islands, but one is omitted from the inclusion in the National Park protection: Madeline Island. This island is the largest of the islands and was omitted due to extensive residential and commercial development already existing on the island.

Since President Nixon established the Apostle Islands as a National Lakeshore in 1970, our recent trip there in 2020 was a milestone as they celebrated their 50th years as a protected site by the National Park Service.

A mecca for lighthouse lovers: the largest
concentration of lighthouses than any
other National Park site.

Having an interest in lighthouses, I really came to the right place:
The Apostle Islands National Lakeshore has a larger concentration of
lighthouses than any other National Park Service site. The Lighthouses
depicted on this poster are the ones scattered among the islands. They
were also listed as a group on the National Register of Historic Places
in 1977 under the name: ***Apostle Islands Lighthouses.*** There are six lighthouses within the Apostle Islands, but there are even more in that area
of Lake Superior, including Ashland Harbor. It's hard to see them all in
one visit, which warrants several trip to the Islands!

17

Chapter 17: Supporting the Parks

In seeking to support the Parks, one of the best ways, and certainly most enjoyable, is to visit them. By becoming more familiar with what the Parks have to offer, you will definitely gain an appreciation for what is out there and chances are very good you will want to explore further. If you decide to pursue supporting the Parks financially, an inspiration to do so would probably be initiated by a visit to at least one of these places that as Americans we treasure.

Bass Harbor Lighthouse-Acadia National Park

The National Park Service offers several different ways to secure passes into the Parks. A new pass program allows Veterans and Gold

Star Families free admission to all the Parks; a wonderful benefit for our Veterans.

In general, visitors to the parks may purchase day use passes (cost depending on the park or site) or a more economical purchase would be an annual pass. The annual pass to the parks, called *: America the Beautiful- National Parks & Federal Recreational Lands Annual Pass*, provides entrance to all of the over 400 National Park Service sites. The Pass is available to everyone. The cost of the annual pass is $80.00.

Seniors (defined as age 62 and up) may visit the Parks with the purchase of a lifetime pass for $80.00. Same cost as the annual pass, but for Seniors it is a lifetime pass. Another advantage of this pass is that traveling companions can also enter for free. Luckily, my husband purchased his at age 62 before the price increase. We sure packed many awesome trips to the Parks with our $10 pass! Nevertheless, it still is a great value at $80. Imagine our delight with our first use of his senior pass with our trip to Yellowstone with our two teen age sons...all for $10. What a great trip!

More information on purchasing these passes can be found at the following web site: *America the Beautiful - National Parks & Federal Recreational Lands Annual Pass | USGS Store*

After memorable Park adventures, many park goers are inspired to support the Parks financially to help assist programs and insure future generations can have access to the same experiences. There are many organizations that provide assistance to the National Park Service however, these three organizations stand out as the major supporters. Throughout the past few years I have belonged to all three of these, at one time or another, so I have firsthand knowledge of their projects and impacts on the Parks. It is interesting to note that several larger Parks like Yosemite, Yellowstone and Glacier for example, have their own foundations that focus entirely on that specific Park. If you have a favorite then you may want to pursue supporting a specific Park.

The National Park Service is primarily funded by **Congress through both the annual appropriations cycle as well as some mandatory funds**. The National Park Service also receives funding through park entrance and user fees, as well as private organizations. These are the three organizations that I wish to highlight that are instrumental in helping the Parks. They help to provide supplemental funding in addition to monies received through Federal funding.

The National Park Foundation.

As the official nonprofit partner of the National Park Service, the National Park Foundation generates private support and builds strategic partnerships to protect and enhance America's national parks for present and future generations.

Many of their efforts seem to be focused on educational endeavors: helping to make Americans  more aware of parks programs and thereby encouraging parks explorations. Their mission statement declares:

"Chartered by Congress in 1967, the National Park Foundation is rooted in a legacy that began more than a century ago, when private citizens from all walks of life took action to establish and protect our national parks. Today, the National Park Foundation carries on that tradition as the only national charitable nonprofit whose mission is to directly support the National Park Service."

It is easy to confuse the National Park Foundation with the National Parks Conservation Association; after all they both work to preserve and enhance our National Parks. Yet, the National Park Foundation is the only organization that is directly affiliated with the NPS.

National Parks Conservation Association

If you are like me, in awe of our nation's National Parks, you must applaud the efforts of the *National Parks Conservation Association*

(NCPA). Since they are a private organization, not directly affiliated directly with the NPS like the National Park Foundation, they have the freedom to act in the political realm to advocate for the Parks. They are involved legislatively on many issues that directly affect the Parks.

Alongside the National Park Service and the National Park Foundation, the NCPA works to protect and preserve the nation's iconic national parks landscapes by alleviating air pollution, restoring and protecting water and wildlife, encouraging responsible oil and mining operations, and preserving the rich history and culture.

The NPCA focuses on broad ecosystem conservation of many landscapes, including Great Smoky Mountains, Canyonlands, and Yellowstone National Parks, and habitat preservation in parks such as Badlands, Grand Teton, and Olympic National Parks.

The Sierra Club Foundation

The Sierra Club Foundation, founded in 1892 by John Muir of the Mountains, has a legacy of growth similar to that of the establishment of the National Park Service. Muir was also instrumental in establishing the model of what a National Park should be.. The Sierra Club initiated the creation of many national parks, including the Grand Canyon, Mt. Rainier, and Glacier National Parks; persuaded Congress to enlarge others, including Sequoia National Park and Grand Teton National Monument; and encouraged the formation of the National Park Service in 1916.

With the support of 2.4 million members, the Sierra Club's **Our Wild America** campaign has been able to protect 250 million acres in the country.

Whichever way you choose to support America's Parks, please find solace in knowing your efforts are appreciated not only today, but for generations to come.

18

Chapter 18-That was then...This is Now

The National Park Service has evolved over its 100+ years existence, with varied perceptions about its role in aiding conservation and recreation. From its humble beginnings as just a vision in Roosevelt's and Muir's mind's eye, the National Park Service has experienced a variety of perspectives, both good and bad, about their mission. Many people, myself included, hold the National Parks Service in high esteem as the folks that help to maintain and protect our beautiful public places in this country. Yet, it's not all blue skies and sunshine. There are almost as many opinions about the NPS and "appropriate" land use as there are plots of land. ***Therein is the heart of where most problems with the National Park Service lie: Land Usage.*** Which begs the question, who should be in charge of a particular area and to what extent? Think about Native Americans that have been "re-located" off their ancestral lands to make room for the white man's hunting grounds or recreation playgrounds. Think about ranchers in the western plains states whose lands are subject to restrictions put in place by the NPS. *There are no easy answers, but as lovers of our lands it's only right that the questions be asked.*

To exacerbate some of the bad perceptions of the National Park Service, they are a branch of the Federal government and with that come partisan politics that frequently divide issues affecting the operation of our Parks and sites. Since the NPS is a predominantly funded by the Federal government operated programs can be affected, either adversely or positively, depending on the current administration. Theodore Roosevelt got the ball rolling as "The Conservation President" and many of the sound conservation programs including the steps for the establishment of the NPS can be attributed to Roosevelt. Then as we look at more recent administrations, Barack Obama passed more legislation to protect lands and establish monuments than any other President. The future of the sanctity and preservation of our most beloved lands is currently threatened under the current administration. Again, the issue frequently comes down to **land usage**. I shudder at the thought that a recent President even considered extending mining rights within the boundaries of the Grand Canyon. Luckily there are enough people who not only love the Parks but also understand the long term ramifications of such actions. Short term economic gains do not justify permanent desecration of some of the most beautiful landscapes in the world.

Point Reyes National Lakeshore

A good example of the complexity of land usage matters is found with Point Reyes National Seashore. The seashore, an hour north of San Francisco, is managed and protected by the NPS. The issues surrounding the management and operation of the land does indeed provide an example of how complicated the issues involving the National

Park Service can become. Yet it also shows how the battles that ensue can become so tragic and intense.

To understand how complex these issues can become, it is best to have a brief overview of the history of Point Reyes. President John F. Kennedy established the National Seashore at Point Reyes in 1962, but the government only owned a portion of the land. The rest of the land in that area had been owned and operated by ranchers and dairy farmers for over 100 years. Much of the land was purchased from the farmers and ranchers with the federal government allowing them to continue farming on the land with long term leases.

The efforts to restore the endangered elk were considered successful. However, the problems that occurred and fights that brewed among conservationists, the National Park Service and the ranchers using the land culminated in several lawsuits. In September of 2020, the NPS released

Sharing the grasslands
(photo:baynature.org)

an impact statement that extends the leases for the ranchers. It also allowed National Park Service rangers to shoot native Tule elk and otherwise drive the elk away from ranch lands. As you can imagine, this plan would make the ranchers happy, but the conservationists who fought so hard to re-populate an endangered species were frustrated and perplexed…to say the least. This push/pull battle on the use of public lands is frequently fought. The decisions made at Point Reyes have been fluctuating for almost the past decade and it is unlikely that the story has come to an end yet.

Since the inception of the National Park Service, issues such as these have surfaced and will more than likely continue to do so. The NPS realizes, perhaps in so many ways, that *you can't please all the people all the time."* They devise general guidelines for smooth operations of the parks and continued goals for conservation. Yet, inevitably situations arise that demand a reexamination of what they believed to be "gospel." As Americans, our perceptions of how the land should be utilized and what we believe makes a beautiful park and/or vacation spot has varied from generation to generation. Some things are quintessential, but some perceptions do change. When I was a kid growing up in the 1960's, it seemed commonplace and *"Oh so much fun!"* to feed the bears at Yellowstone from your car window. We know better now...not good for the bears or the people. Yet, the NPS has strived to meet those needs of a changing America and at the same time assuring the conservation of our most sacred lands.

Fast forward to 2020; a look at the devastating Corona virus that swept through our country shows it had profound impacts on our society. The number of deaths was staggering and how the virus impacted every aspect of our lives. As the increased demands on the public to isolate and *"shelter in place"*, so did our need to get outside, get some fresh air and enjoy the beauty of a park. Park attendance increased dramatically, which was good news for increasing the public's awareness of the splendor of our public landscapes, but became an added challenge to the Park administrators to handle the crowds and keep park goers safe during one of the most devastating pandemics this country has seen.

At one point during 2020, some of the Parks and sites had to temporarily close to visitors to help contain the spread of the virus. The NPS helped to keep everyone informed of closures and restrictions, which was a challenge because the situation frequently changed. As many organizations did, the NPS promoted many reminders for mask wearing in public places, hand washing and social-distancing. Here is a sample of one of their reminders for social-distancing. A little levity helps the situation and still makes a point:

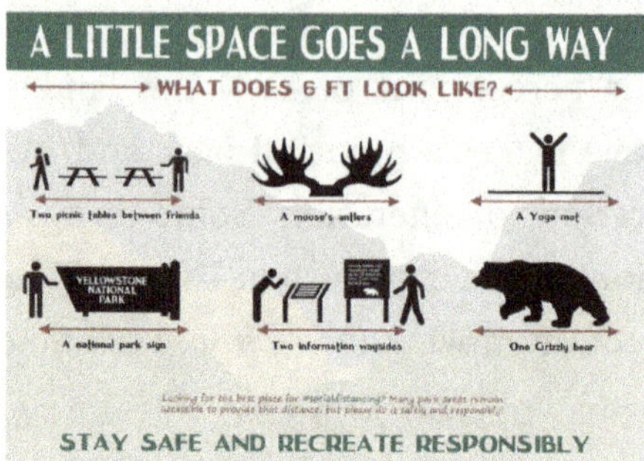

Poster from the National Park Service,
2020 pandemic

My trip to the Utah parks in the fall of 2020 almost didn't happen and the plans I made were subject to change at a moment's notice. Zion had closed several trails, campgrounds and the shuttle service in March. The Park remained opened but with limited access

The view on the Watchman Trail @ Zion
National Park

The shuttle system did reopen in July, but with a new ticketing system that assured 50% capacity on the buses to maintain social distancing. It was a good system, but nevertheless seemed awkward when visitors to the park were seeking wide open spaces. At this particular point in time, it would have been nice to go somewhere "mask free." Yet, I gave the NPS great credit for making the best of a bad situation; the pandemic was bad enough….thank goodness we could still get out and enjoy the Parks even if it was very different than the usual Park experience. It appeared to me, that a great majority of the Park goers did their very best they could to follow the rules in the spirit of cooperation and relishing the opportunity to enjoy the unique beauty of Zion National Park.

Waiting for the Shuttle at Zion: with masks and social distancing

So our trip to Zion was incredible, in spite of the pandemic regulations that gave the trip some "unique" qualities. Qualities that will indeed make it memorable.

Another element that made the Zion trip stick out in my mind is how the NPS handled the pandemic; a positive perception in my mind. It seemed to me that the NPS did everything they could to provide a safe environment for visitors, but also realized the importance of connecting with nature and seeking the great outdoors at a time when the whole nation was just about going crazy with all the quarantine policies.

Getting ready to hike "The Narrows" at Zion.

John Muir knew the healing powers of nature when he said:

"Thousands of tired, nerve-shaken, over-civilized people are beginning to find out that going to the mountains is going home; that wildness is a necessity; and that mountain parks and reservations are useful not only as fountains of timber and irrigating rivers, but as fountains of life."

So John Muir had it right…we need the wilderness to restore our souls and renew our spirits. Whatever your perceptions of the National Parks may be, or perhaps you don't have an opinion one way or the other….take the time to see what the National Park Service has to offer. Seeking out a few hours or perhaps an extended trip to a Park can be well worth the effort. Even if it's as simple as a *"Walk in the Park"*.

Julie E. Smith

Further Reading/Sources

1. Brinkley, Douglas, *The Wilderness Warrior Theodore Roosevelt and the Crusade for America.* HarperCollins Publishers(2009)

2. Burns, Ken and D. Duncan. *The National Parks America's Best Idea*, RR Donnelley(2011)

3. Cronon, William, *Uncommon Ground, Rethinking the Human Place in Nature*, W.W.Norton & Company(1996)

4. Eyewitness Travel Guide, *Alaska*, Dorling Kindersley Limited (2012)

5. National Geographic, *Guide to National Parks of the United States*, Seventh Edition. (2012)

6. The National Park Service is a very reliable source for getting complete information when planning a trip. The site is divided by state and provides current information on necessary tips to make your trip a success. The site is: **www.nps.gov**

To read more of Julie's writing on a variety of topics, in addition to travel, check out her blog at: julieetta1982.blogspot.com entitled: **Outlooks and Inspirations**

About the Author

Julie is a free-lance writer with a passion for the Parks, and additional sites managed by the National Park Service. Her desire is to show others all the fantastic adventures that are available through the National Park Service.

**Julie visiting Bryce Canyon
National Park, Utah**

Her hobbies include photography and scrapbooking. Trips to the Parks provide ample opportunities to document the parks in pictures.

Julie was born and raised in Des Moines, Iowa and received her degree in Journalism at the University of Iowa. She and her husband live in the beautiful north woods of Wisconsin and delight in travel to the great outdoors whenever they can.

www.ingramcontent.com/pod-product-compliance
Lightning Source LLC
Chambersburg PA
CBHW061034050726
47592CB00004B/1431